The B____
Guide to

THRIVING

Fruit that will last

ANCIENT PATHWAYS
to personal freedom

FOR DEEPER ROOTS

Rob Cresswell

The Believer's Guide to Thriving

© Copyright 2022 – Rob Cresswell

All Scripture quotations are taken from the New International Version © 1973, 1978, 1984 by International Bible Society.

ISBN: 9780957264274

Visit: SpiritLifestyle.com

Contact: info@SpiritLifestyle.com

Contents

page

Making the most of this book

This book is written as a practical guide to help the reader cultivate a healthy devotional lifestyle. Each chapter ends with an activation which can be used to practise the devotion in question.

I recommend that you allow some time between reading each chapter to do the activation. That way you will learn most effectively before moving on to the next one.

There is an optional video series to accompany this book on **SpiritLifestyle.com**

introduction

In my first book, '**The Believer's Guide to Survival**' I laid out five essentials for Christian life. This was written as a 'pocket guide' for new believers, to establish basic principles upon which to build a faith life on the foundation of the gospel of Jesus. Using the analogy of essentials for the physical body (air, water, food etc) we looked at relationship with God, continually being filled with the Holy Spirit, getting to know the Bible, spiritual protection, godly purpose and the value of engaging in Christian community.

So now, having established a good beginning let's turn our sights towards growth and maturity:

"Therefore let us leave the elementary doctrine of Christ and go on to maturity, not laying again a foundation of repentance from dead works and of faith toward God..." Hebrews 6:1

In this book '**The Believer's Guide to Thriving**' we're going to be working through a section of Jesus' 'Sermon on the Mount' in **Matthew chapter 6**. In this teaching,

Jesus instructs us about the value of the personal or private disciplines of charity, prayer and fasting. Using Jesus' teaching on heavenly treasure and also not worrying about the future, I have also included the Christian devotions of worship and meditation.

In a sense the more we mature in Christ the more child-like our faith becomes. We may develop certain 'skills' in these disciplines but (if handled rightly) they will only teach us more about the depth of God's grace and our great dependence on Him.

At heart, the personal disciplines are to train us to excel in submission to God and the goal of this is to allow the Lord to do His transforming work in our hearts. In time, the fruit of this work will begin to manifest in our lives, touching our character, values, relationships and all we endeavour to do. I hope this book is a blessing to you as you seek to know the depths of God's grace and love in your life.

"Stand at the crossroads and look; ask for the ancient paths, ask where the good way is, and walk in it, and you will find rest for your souls." Jeremiah 6:16

Chapter 1

soul garden

the challenge of grace

Here's the basic faith-leap of Christianity: The corner-stone of the gospel is that we're saved by the grace of God and not by our own efforts or righteousness. This is made possible by the atoning sacrifice of Jesus, the lamb of God who takes away the sin of the world[a]. As Jesus himself explained to Nicodemus:

"Just as Moses lifted up the snake in the wilderness, so the Son of Man must be lifted up, that everyone who believes may have eternal life in him." John 3:14

The eternal salvation of our soul is offered freely by the sacrifice of Jesus and received through faith. Take a moment to receive that truth and revel in the wonder of it... Now this changes everything. Once we have

a John 1:29

placed our faith in Jesus as our Saviour, we are set free. Now we don't measure our righteousness by the good works we do; now we consider ourselves righteous (acceptable to God) by the righteousness of Jesus. This is not simply the 'good news' of the gospel but the extremely amazing news because Jesus is wholly righteous, and by faith in Him, so are we.

"God made him who had no sin to be sin for us, so that in him we might become the righteousness of God." 2 Corinthians 5:21

This outrageous message of the gospel teaches us that now we are empowered to do good *because* Jesus has made us righteous. Our motivation for doing good now comes out of a supernaturally transformed heart. It's an inside job! This is a massive paradigm shift for our outlook on life. We used to think we did good deeds (give to the poor, help the needy, etc.) to become more righteous (get in God's good books). But now we do them because we're already in God's good books! This is what sets Christianity apart from all other religions or 'ways of life'. We may all have 'doing good' in common, but we are motivated to do so for entirely different reasons. Essentially, it's what makes Christianity a 'faith' (and uniquely a faith in a person), rather than a religion or a 'way of life'. It's not *what* we do, it's *why* we do it.

So, this surely begs the question, doesn't it? When it comes to the Christian faith what place is there for effort, or work, or sacrifice? Since Jesus has done it all anyway. Is there any at all? What if I don't feel like praying or serving the Lord today? What difference does it make to my salvation? Is there any value in making myself do these things? Because, and here's the dilemma, once I do things, not out of love and gratitude to Jesus, but rather, 'because I think I ought to do them' then surely I'm back to that 'trying to be good by my own (dead) works'[a] again; and there's no longer any real value in doing that... is there?

A GUARD AGAINST WEAKNESS

Now everything in us should think, "Hang on, no, that's not right, we can't live our lives by how we feel, that's a shallow and selfish way to live; it's unspiritual." But sadly, this is exactly the sort of mind-set many Christians end up with. It's what Dietrich Bonhoeffer referred to as 'cheap grace':

"The essence of grace, we suppose, is that the account has been paid in advance; and, because it has been paid, everything can be had for nothing... Cheap grace is grace without discipleship, grace without the cross, grace without Jesus Christ, living and incarnate."[b]

a Hebrew 6:1, b 'The Cost of Discipleship' Bonhoeffer

If we conclude that this gospel of grace leaves no room for sacrifice or self-discipline then the real problem is with our thinking, not with the gospel.

But watch out! Don't start making a list of duties just yet. There were those in the early church who were determined to impose external rules and regulations on new believers, but the Apostle Paul addresses them too. He says they are trying to rob the cross of its power. He explains that outward acts of religion now count for nothing in the light of God's grace. What counts is inner spiritual transformation of the heart and mind:

"Such restrictions indeed have an appearance of wisdom, with their self-prescribed worship, their false humility, and their harsh treatment of the body; but they are of no value against the indulgence of the flesh." Colossians 2:23

The Apostle Paul not only had to address those who wanted to impose a 'do whatever you like immorality' on new Christians, he also had to correct those who swung the other way with lists of harsh rules, disciplines and regulations. So, which is it to be? Self-discipline or no self-discipline? The answer is in the balance that makes a third way; a narrow way.

THE NARROW WAY

The ancient paths of Christian devotion are the narrow way between empty works and immoral licence or between self-righteousness and self-serving laziness. They hold in balance sacrifice and grace, obedience and devotion, obligation and whole-hearted consent.

There is a spiritual battle going on after all. There are forces in our lives that seek to rob us of the freedom of the gospel, not least: the world, the flesh and the devil[a]. The real value of the disciplines is that they help to strengthen our faith in this fight and help us 'work out our salvation'[b]. Through faith in the gospel of grace we can walk in meaningful self-discipline and a real passion for the things of the Spirit.

"This is what the LORD says: 'Stand at the crossroads and look; ask for the ancient paths, ask where the good way is, and walk in it, and you will find rest for your souls.'" Jeremiah 6:16

The 'ancient pathway' is the low road to the highway that saints have walked before us and beckon all those who seek the deeper life to follow. We are, after all, called to be disciples and the word 'disciple' comes from the same root as the word 'discipline'. The reason we practice self-control, (which is a fruit of the Holy

a Ephesians 2:2-3 and 1 John 2:15-17, b Philippians 2:12

Spirit[a]), is because we have submitted control of our lives to Jesus. The determination to practice spiritual devotions on a regular basis guards against the danger of our human weaknesses (only pursuing the things of God when it suits me, or using God's grace as an excuse to be self-centred). They can prevent us from being shallow or fickle in our faith, and they can and will help us cultivate a passion for God by transforming our thinking and helping us mature spiritually.

GETTING OFF THE SCALES

The Apostle Paul often uses the terms of slavery or imprisonment to convey spiritual truths about our salvation. In his letter to the young church in Rome he names two particular slave drivers as 'the law' and 'the flesh'.

"So then, I myself in my mind am a slave to God's law, but in my sinful nature (or the flesh) a slave to the law of sin." Romans 7:25

He summarises our pre-salvation dilemma like this: *'The law punishes me when I'm bad and the flesh punishes me when I'm good. So, I can't win.'* The problem is that these two task masters inevitably create a 'scales-of-balance' mentality that shackles my thinking.

a Galatians 5:23

Imagine an old-fashioned pair of kitchen scales with a tin plate on each side and a pivot in the middle. If I'm selfish and overindulge my flesh, in my thinking the scales tip one way. Now I'm in debt to my heavenly bank account, 'I'm in the red' so to speak. Now I feel guilty and need to make restoration so I feel compelled to address the balance. So, let's see, I'll do a few random acts of kindness, maybe give to charity and go to a church prayer meeting... and there! We're good with God again! And mistakenly, in my thinking, I'm all set for a bit more self-indulgence.

That's how most people in the world live. And sadly, it's how many Christians live too... the tragedy is that in reality (according to the gospel), Jesus has set us free from that kind of lifestyle. However, many of us still settle for thinking and living that way. It's a worldly mind-set that we have to allow the Holy Spirit to break off us and replace with a mind-set of divine love[a].

PRISON BREAK

Have you ever seen the movie, The Shawshank Redemption? It's a pretty gritty movie (and not for everyone), but it's one of the most popular movies ever made[b]. It's about the long-term imprisonment of an innocent man called Andy Dufresne in Portland Maine, Shawshank

a Romans 12, b Impressively remaining at the very top of the IMDB 100

State Penitentiary. It's a tale of endurance and patience, but it's also about how long-term prisoners can become institutionalised in the prison system.

Those 'lifers' who entered the prison as young men may leave as old men. Prison life is all they know; and often they're simply not equipped for life on the outside. They can't cope with their 'freedom' and they're lost and vulnerable without rules and regulations. The tragedy is that those who are released often reoffend 'on the outside' so they can go back to the prison life they know.

This is a picture of what happens to so many of us when Jesus sets us free from the prison of the law and the flesh. Despite our hatred of the prison and all it stands for, we're deeply institutionalised; we don't know how else to think. So, we're often tempted to sabotage our 'freedom in Christ' and go back to that 'scales of balance' mentality. Even our church life can reinforce this behaviour as we fall into habitual sins through the week and get saved again every Sunday. Jesus died to get us off this roundabout and onto a journey of freedom to a transformed mind and spiritual maturity.

FIVE SECRET DEVOTIONS

This is where the spiritual disciplines can have an

important role to play. A personal commitment to observe regular disciplined observances, such as fasting or giving, can help position us to receive the renewing work of the Holy Spirit in our minds. Remember that though we may invest the time and effort, it's the Holy Spirit who's doing the real work of inner transformation. What the disciplines do is help reorientate us in our attitudes and thinking to receive His inner work. This is what Jesus meant by having 'eyes that are good'[a] and what Paul meant by being 'transformed by the renewing of your mind'[b].

These are ancient pathways that are well trodden by the host of saints who have gone before us, who encourage us to walk these paths of humility and self-control, of love and devotion with a legacy of devotional books. St John of the cross wrote 'The Imitation of Christ', Jean Guyon wrote, 'A method of prayer' and Brother Lawrence wrote letters compiled into a collection called 'Practicing the presence of God'. They were all discovering just how deeply they could journey into the depths of God through the personal devotions.

In this book we're going to look at five devotional disciplines based on part of Jesus' sermon on the mount in Matthew chapter 6. They are charity, prayer, fasting, worship, and meditation. There is a place for

a Matthew 6:22, b Romans 12:2

disciplines to be expressed in and with community, but in this book we're going to focus on personal or private devotions. They're just between you and God; nobody needs to know about them. In fact, Jesus teaches us that it's better if they don't. These devotions should be guarded like special intimacies between lovers; as far as anybody else is concerned - it's none of their business!

THE ART OF PRACTISING

We would do well to bring the same attitudes of learning to spirituality as we do to other types of learning. Few of us have difficulty understanding what it takes to be truly proficient at a sport, a craft or a musical instrument. If we are serious about gaining mastery at any pursuit, we will ready ourselves for the thrill of new skills, achieving short term goals and also for the long haul.

Here's a few of the basic principles:

1. Shorter, regular practices are better than longer more sporadic practice sessions

2. It's better to focus on weaknesses than spend a lot of time doing what you already know

3. Planning goals and record keeping help motivate us and monitor progress

Let's bear this in mind as we prepare ourselves for learning these devotions with the Holy Spirit.

A WORD OF WARNING

Before we embark on our devotional journey, I want to state clearly that these spiritual disciplines are never a substitute for obedience to the Holy Spirit (that's the old 'law and the flesh prison thinking'). Obedience is always better than sacrifice[a]. Neither will they fix deep seated issues of addiction or compulsive behaviour if approached in the wrong way; in fact they may make them worse. What the Christian disciplines will do, if handled rightly, is help to position us more readily in a posture of true humility to receive the guidance and transforming work of the Holy Spirit.

TENDING THE SOUL GARDEN

Many of us suffer from what we might call the tyranny of the instant. Instant entertainment, fast food, instant service, instant credit. However, if we bring this expectation for 'instant' to aspects of our spiritual growth, we'll have a problem. Investment in spiritual growth needs a long-term approach.

Think of a beautiful garden. Day to day you may hardly notice any change. In fact, there may be seasons where

a 1 Samuel 15:22

all the growth is taking place underground and out of sight. Sometimes areas of the garden have to look worse before they get better, but the long-term result is full grown and stunning.

There is no such thing as an instant devotional life. When God created mankind He put them in a wonderful garden and told them to look after it. In the same way, we have a mandate under God to take care of the spiritual garden of our lives. This isn't meant to be meaningless toil, but purposeful, rewarding labour; God wants us to partner with Him to cultivate the inner world of our lives so that we can enjoy it together.

NURTURING THE DIVINE LIFE

The Bible says that when we are born again, we're born of the Holy Spirit. This means that our whole spiritual DNA has changed. It means that we're born of imperishable seed; seed that contains everything we need for life and health and godliness.

"For you have been born again, not of perishable seed, but of imperishable, through the living and enduring word of God." 1 Peter 1:23

It also means that we have a new purpose: to make sure that the germinating seed that God has planted in our lives through faith is looked after and nurtured by every means we have.

Have you ever grown a new plant from seed? We can get protective of it can't we? We'll use every means we have to nurture it and optimise its potential; water, food, bug killers, netting and support canes. We keep checking it because everything in us wants that tiny plant to flourish and grow. We notice with a thrill every new leaf and millimetre of growth. It's only a seedling but we set our sights on the mature tree or shrub that will give us so much future joy with flowers and fruit.

WORKING WITH THE MASTER GARDENER

If your life is like a garden, then the Lord Jesus is your master gardener. He has designed the blueprint for your life, and he knows what kind of garden he intends your life to be. It will have paths, places to sit, places to play, places to be fruitful, water features and seating areas and many wonderful hidden corners that look and smell amazing.

This is our inner sanctuary, 'the secret place', the spiritual garden of our lives. The dwelling place of God[a]. The personal disciplines are like tools that help us tend the garden of our soul. This devotional work goes on without anybody else being involved; it's a

a 1 Corinthians 6:19

work of intimacy between you and the Holy Spirit. And in time, the fruit of your devotional times will be a blessing to others. It may even take them by surprise. Because what happens over time is that the garden grows according to God's plans and purposes[a]. We become transformed on the inside, into the image of Jesus, without even realising it, because the life that thrives and blossoms is the work of God[b].

a 1 Corinthians 3:7, b Philippians 1:6

ACTIVATION

For this exploration of the devotional life we will be using Matthew chapter 6 as our key scripture.

To prepare for this, read Matthew Chapter 6 all the way through. Get familiar with it by reading it 2 or 3 times. See if the Lord is drawing your attention to certain parts of the chapter. Perhaps try memorising a verse, carry it with you and try recalling it during your day.

Chapter 2

charity

the overflowing life

In Matthew chapter 6 Jesus teaches us not to use our generosity to impress others.

"So when you give to the needy, do not announce it with trumpets, as the hypocrites do in the synagogues and on the streets, to be honoured by others. Truly I tell you, they have received their reward in full. But when you give to the needy, do not let your left hand know what your right hand is doing, so that your giving may be in secret. Then your Father, who sees what is done in secret, will reward you." Matthew 6:2-4

This is the first of several instructions Jesus gave us for our private devotions to God and it concerns the giving of money to help others. The topic of money is vast in its scope, but for our purposes we want to focus on our personal generosity and how we can use it to serve God with integrity.

SACRIFICIAL LOVE

The primary fruit of the Spirit that will develop in our lives through the devotion of giving is divine or sacrificial love. Traditionally the word 'charity' was used to describe this kind of love and it is deeply connected to the discipline of giving. However, to the modern mind the word 'charity' refers to an organisation that seeks to be of public benefit (and gives tax breaks). But long before it was commandeered by 'not for profit' organisations, the original definition of charity was "Christian love in its highest manifestation" and its Latin version (caritas) was used in early translations of the Bible for the Greek word 'agape'.

Divine love is not the same as emotional or romantic love. Divine love is a fruit of the Holy Spirit and is formed in a person's character through obedience and service to God. In contrast, other types of love (for example: self-love, romantic love, or obsessive love) are much more volatile and based on complex psychological and social circumstances. It's easy to confuse divine love with other types of love because emotional love can feel so deep and powerful, but they are fundamentally different (for a superb definition of divine love read 1 Corinthians 13). It's good to remember this difference as we discuss the devotion of charity because it's the formation of godly character and values within us, rather than a desire or feeling that may come and go.

FREELY GIVE

Before Jesus sent out his disciples to go and minister to others with the message and power of the Kingdom, He told them:

"Freely you have received; freely give." Matthew 10:8

As recipients of grace (unearned favour) the Lord expects us to be dispensers of grace; a generous people. Speaking of the Holy Spirit, Jesus said that out of our innermost being rivers of water would over-flow[a]. This is a picture of a soul that is receiving too much to hold; a soul that is overflowing with God's love and goodness.

Now, our external circumstances may not appear to reflect this truth because we all go through extremely rough and tough times. However, we must not base our inner gratitude solely on external circumstances, because to do so would be worldly (pursuing material

a John 7:38

pleasure for its own sake). After all, our perception of need is often relative, and one man's 'poor' is another man's 'rich'. Rather, the discipline of giving and receiving is practised primarily through faith and often despite our circumstances.

The devotional discipline of charity or divine love is twofold. It's about receiving and giving. It has to firstly be about receiving from God (I'm not speaking only of material things here), because if we attempt to give without receiving, we will simply dry up. But as we do receive it's also about the discipline of allowing that life to overflow to others, otherwise the life in us will simply stagnate.

MONEY MATTERS

Many are reluctant to talk about money. In Britain people will rarely reveal their income in conversation because we feel it reveals our status and makes us vulnerable. And then for many the whole notion of managing finances is almost laughable. "What finances?", you might say, "I don't have finances, I have debts!" Now, believe me, we've been there and it's no joke to be in money difficulties, but we must never allow those circumstances to sour our heart towards giving. Even if we have no money, we can always give our time.

In truth, when I say 'managing our finances' I'm not talking about accounting and budgeting, although that is no bad thing. I'm talking about managing the way we think about our finances. It's possible to be relatively cash poor but very prosperous by the Bible's definition of prosperity; walking in gratitude, peace, joy and love. And by the same token we all know that it's perfectly possible to be cash rich and desperately impoverished in these commodities.

There is a spirit of poverty that has nothing to do with material wealth but everything to do with a poverty of the soul. Many who are deemed poor in the west are relatively rich by world standards of poverty, however, there is a spirit of poverty and entitlement that keeps many trapped in a perception of lack.

A CALL TO STEWARDSHIP

In the gospels when Jesus teaches us about the subject of money He often frames it in the context of good stewardship. As we lay down our lives in our private devotions to the Lord we remind ourselves that all we have is His, and this includes our time and money. When we commit the day to Him we ask if the Lord will help us to use the resources we have primarily for His purposes. Now, 'His purposes' includes our responsibilities towards ourselves and our family (especially spouse and dependents), but it may also include many other possibilities, when we begin to open up to them.

A primary benefit of stewarding our resources well is that it helps us to not be manipulated by external pressures to give. Charity fund-raisers know that if they put an image of a beautiful wide-eyed girl at the end of their TV advert that they will raise substantially more than if they use an image of an elderly man. Most of the time we are responsive givers; we give when we are asked. That's why so many charities spend large percentages of their income on advertising and fund-raising. That's not always a bad thing. God wants us to be a compassionate and merciful people who respond well to need. But in this devotion we are actively looking to the guidance of the Holy Spirit to direct us (in advance of requests) in how to serve and give.

WHEN YOU GIVE TO THE NEEDY

As with all the personal devotions, God is looking for those who are serious about serving Him. This isn't about 'your ministry' or 'evangelism' or 'outreach'; it's about deepening your relationship with God. In Matthew 25 Jesus tells of the end of the age when **'the Son of Man comes in His glory'**. He says He will sort out the people to the left and the right:

"Then the King will say to those on His right, 'Come, you who are blessed by my Father; take your inheritance, the kingdom prepared for you since the creation of the world. For I was hungry and you gave me something to eat, I was thirsty and you gave me something to drink, I was a stranger and you invited me in, I needed clothes and you clothed me, I was sick and you looked after me, I was in prison and you came to visit me.'" Matthew 25:34-36

The surprise to these people is that they can't remember doing any of these things until they are told:

'Truly I tell you, whatever you did for one of the least of these brothers and sisters of mine, you did for me.'

Challenging words! So often our ideas of giving are clean and clinical, devoid of the complications of relationships with real people. However, in this discipline God is also looking to push our personal boundaries and comfort zones. The need for reaching out to others with practical help is becoming more and more important in our world of economic uncertainty. The devotion of giving is more than simply transferring funds; it's also the sharing of life.

A JOYFUL GIVER

Let's consider the private devotion of selfless giving in regard to our 'soul garden'. In Genesis we see a picture of what this may be like from the Garden of Eden.

"Now a river went out of Eden to water the garden, and from there it parted and became four riverheads." Genesis 2:10

This river of life flowing out of Eden not only waters the garden but then also separates and flows out through rich lands of gold and precious stones. This surely speaks to us of the way in which our heavenly Father will use our generosity of heart to enrich both ourselves and others.

It's only in this context that we can understand what scripture means by a joyful giver. We give joyfully because the very act of giving imparts life into our souls. Just like waterfalls, fountains and overflowing bowls, when we give it isn't something God has to prise out of our fingers, it's actually a joyful expression of an overflowing heart.

CULTIVATING THE DEVOTION OF GIVING

So how can we apply ourselves to this devotion of secret giving? Firstly, by reiterating our total surrender to the Lord. Here's a practical suggestion: Take out your purse or wallet and lay it down in front of you. Say to the Lord, "All I have needed your hand has provided" and, "help me to use my money, my time, my attention and my generosity, to be faithful to you today."

Why not consider inventive ways in which you can give 'in secret'. This is actually very challenging in this age of smart phones and digital banking. It may even mean using cash and not declaring it on tax benefits; but that can be all part of the challenge.

Here's a few suggestions of how we can give in private (not exhaustive and I'm sure you can think of some of your own):

- Send cash to someone through the post. Write a note saying 'Praise God, He is good!' on it (or words to that effect).

- Leave some cash to bless the next person in line with a coffee, particularly if they havn't arrived yet. Recently a couple of students came into our café and one of them told us they'd gone off religion and didn't want prayer. However, without them knowing, a lady they had never met paid for their bill as she left. When the students got up to pay, they were amazed at what had happened; they couldn't get over it. The love of God had impacted them in a way which they would remember for a long time.

- Give anonymously to a good cause or charity that you have no vested interest in.

- Have you ever written to or visited someone in prison? There are organisations to help you do this. For many prisoners this is a life-line.

- Support your local Food Bank by donating food goods.

- Consider setting aside a regular sum of money, no matter how big or small, for the purpose of giving away. In this way you will be actively seeking ways to bless people with it.

THE PRIVATE DISCIPLINE OF GIVING

As with all the other disciplines there is plenty of room for expressions of giving in a corporate context and we should enjoy those too. What 'secret giving' does on a personal level is to set us free from using even our generosity to be self-serving. Our expressions of giving may seem small and trivial, but we must start somewhere, and God can do mighty things with someone who is willing to share their lunch (particularly if it is loaves and fishes!).

Devotional giving helps the life-giving water features in the garden of our lives to flow in, and flow out; to be a blessing to others, with no strings attached.

The promise of Jesus is that if our acts of giving are from the heart and genuinely devoted to God then our heavenly Father will bless us openly. We should have no expectation of what that may look like (we are not trading with God in any devotion), but just a simple trust that if we **"Seek first the Kingdom of God"**[a] then our Heavenly Father will do what is best for us.

"Give, and it will be given to you. A good measure, pressed down, shaken together and running over, will be poured into your lap." Luke 6:38

That's the kind of God we serve.

a Matthew 6:33

ACTIVATION

Earlier on in the chapter I suggested that one way to specifically target submitting the area of personal finances to God was to do a symbolic act of worship with our wallet or purse (or whatever best represents your finances). If you havn't already done this I encourage you to do so; it's a very powerful act of submission:

Take out your purse or wallet and lay it down in front of you. Open your hands, palm upwards, and say to the Lord, *"I thank you for all my finances, and I acknowledge that all I have is from your gracious provision. Such as they are, I offer them up in your service as you help me to be generous with my money, time, and attention. Guide me and give me the wisdom to use my finances well today and every day. In Jesus name, Amen."*

Chapter 3

prayer

the secret groves

As a child I was taught how to pray in school: "Put your hands together and close your eyes". Then the teacher would read a prayer. Having hands together and eyes closed stopped us getting distracted and fidgeting. But woe betide you if you peeped at your friend and got the giggles!

Another early memory I have of prayer is when my family attended a small village Methodist church. A local farmer would pray when he arrived in his pew. He looked very serious as he put his head in his hand for a good five minutes of silent prayer before each Sunday service began.

Most people, even non-believers, pray when they run

out of other options. In this sense prayer is often a last resort. We've tried everything else; I guess we better pray. Someone we love is desperately ill or we just had some bad news, or how about the pilot of our plane has just announced that an engine has failed! This can make even the most ardent atheists pray: 'if you get me out of this God, I'll serve you for the rest of my life...'

Putting it simply, prayer is how we talk to God. When and how we desire to do this is up to us.

PRAYER TRADITIONS

Methods of Christian prayer can vary greatly around the world between cultures and traditions. Prayer can be very ritualised and read out loud at certain times of the day along with candles and incense. The Anglican Church published the Book of Common Prayer in 1549 and has used it ever since; though the 'King James' style language has been updated several times. It contains prayers to be read throughout the church day, prayers for ceremonies such as funerals and also prayers that follow the church calendar throughout the year.

In Judaism there are three main prayer times through-out the day:

Shaharit - daily morning prayers, Mincha - afternoon

prayer (often prayed in a work break), and Maariv - afternoon or night prayers.

Many Christian ecclesiastical traditions reflect this Jewish observation by reciting the Psalms as prayers. Some monastic traditions follow a daily rigorous prayer timetable:

2 am - Matins

3 am - Lauds

6 am - Prime

10 am - Tierce

12 noon - Sext

3 pm - Nones

6 pm - Vespers

8 pm - Compline

12 Midnight - Vigils

It makes you wonder how they get any sleep!

DEVOTIONAL PRAYER

In Matthew 6 Jesus teaches us once again about our devotional life, but this time it's prayer. He tells us not to pray to gain recognition from other people but to pray in secret. Then he says our heavenly Father will reward us.

"And when you pray, do not be like the hypocrites, for they love to pray standing in the synagogues and on the street corners to be seen by others. Truly I tell you, they have received their reward in full. But when you pray, go into your room, close the door and pray to your Father, who is unseen. Then your Father, who sees what is done in secret, will reward you."
Matthew 6:5-6

Jesus doesn't say *if* you pray but *when* you pray, so we can be sure that this should be a normal part of the believer's life. Notice also that Jesus isn't instructing us to go to the temple, but to find a quiet place of solitude in our own home, the place where we live. Jesus was consumed with passion for the Jewish temple when He turned over the traders' tables and shouted **"...my house will be called a house of prayer for all nations."**[a] So when Jesus tells us to pray at home He's telling us our life should be a house of prayer; a place for communion with God.

After all, we are told in Genesis 3 that God walked and communed with Adam and Eve in the garden in the cool of the day. Could this be what God intends for us in the devotional time of our soul garden?

a Matthew 21:13

A ROYAL PRIESTHOOD

In Old Testament times priests would burn incense on the golden altar that sat just before the curtain separating the Holy Place from the Holy of Holies. They would burn the heavily perfumed incense every morning and every evening. It was a symbol of the prayers of intercession that would go before God as a sweet fragrance. In Revelation 8 we read:

"An angel was given much incense to offer, with the prayers of all God's people, on the golden altar in front of the throne. The smoke of the incense, together with the prayers of God's people, went up before God from the angel's hand."

We must remember that for the believer it is Jesus Himself who is our great intercessor[a] and it is through Him that we can boldly approach the throne of grace with our prayers of thanksgiving, intercession and worship[b]. We are a royal priesthood. We have the ear of the King, and can offer prayers before God as those sanctified by our high priest Jesus. This is the high calling of prayer to the believer.

HOW TO PRAY

Jesus taught us how to pray:

a Romans 8:34, b Hebrews 4:16

"This, then, is how you should pray:

He said start prayer in a way which places the emphasis on our relationship with God as our Father:

"'Our Father in heaven, hallowed be your name."

Then an affirmation of our submission and agreement with His purpose and will:

"Your kingdom come, your will be done, on earth as it is in heaven."

This leads us to ask for enough provision for today:

"Give us today our daily bread."

And then to recognise His mercy to us through Jesus - and subsequently our mercy to others:

"And forgive us our debts, as we also have forgiven our debtors."

And finally we ask for the help and protection we know He is willing to give:

"And lead us not into a time of testing but deliver us from evil."

And finally to end our prayers with adoration and worship:

"For yours is the Kingdom, the power and the glory - forever and ever Amen."

In summary, Jesus' model for devotional prayer includes articulating:

- Identity & relationship
- Submission
- Purpose
- Provision
- Forgiveness and redemptive life-flow
- Protection
- Adoration

FORGIVENESS

Not only does Jesus' model for devotional prayer contain a pivotal theme of forgiveness, Jesus then goes on to emphasise how essential this aspect of effective prayer is:

"For if you forgive other people when they sin against you, your heavenly Father will also forgive you. But if you do not forgive others their sins, your Father will not forgive your sins." Matthew 6:14-15

Does that sound harsh to you? We don't like reading that there may be circumstances in which God won't forgive us do we? But this tells us about the nature of forgiveness. The receiving of forgiveness necessitates the releasing of it. It's the same principle that we saw in the previous chapter about giving and receiving.

It's a mistake to think of forgiveness as if it is a static, inanimate thing. Forgiveness is about relationship and relationships don't stand still; they move (grow, change, and develop). The forgiveness of God brings us a future that's alive with the Holy Spirit; it has a life-flow. Jesus is saying that in order to receive that flow or release of forgiveness we must also let go of our own offenses. Forgiveness needs to run through us like a river through the garden of our soul.

Jesus teaches us that forgiveness (receiving it and releasing others) is essential if we are going to live in freedom. If you are struggling with forgiveness issues, ask the Holy Spirit to help you let go and forgive; one step at a time. You'll be so glad you did.

THE DISCIPLINE OF PERSONAL PRAYER

We need to make room in our lives for prayer. We can get blasé about prayer and imagine that those little thoughts that pop in our heads during other activities are a sufficient prayer life, but these are no substitute for purposefully setting time aside to stop other activities and enter into a more fully engaged time of communing with our heavenly Father. In **Luke 5:15** we read:

"Yet the news about Him spread all the more, so that crowds of people came to hear Him and to be healed of their sicknesses. But Jesus often withdrew to lonely places and prayed."

When Jesus said, **"Go into your room and shut the door"**, this can mean different things for different people. For Jesus it was often outdoor places of solitude like the Garden of Gethsemane[a] (an olive grove in the Kidron Valley) or up in the hills[b]. Consider making a quiet corner in your home a praying space. It could be an armchair in the attic room, a bean bag in your room, or a window seat. I know many Christians who love sitting in a place they can see some sky or garden. When I was younger for me to 'close the door' was to go out into the fields. If you have a young family and a very busy life, praying while walking the dog, or on your commute can work well too.

As Jesus taught us, start with thanksgiving and an acknowledgement of who God is, and who He is to you, is often a good place to start. Praying out loud is good too. It may feel odd to do that on your own, but it really

a Matthew 26:36, b Luke 6:12

helps us to articulate and focus our thoughts.

I vividly remember a prayer experience after I had been running away from the Lord for some years during my teens. I was counselled by an older friend to find a quiet place and talk to God. He said, 'Just tell him where you've been'.

It was the strangest thing sitting there under a tree in Wales on my own. I said, "Hello God. It's me, Rob..." It felt very odd, but that was the beginning of a wonderful 'returning son' experience for me. Praying your thoughts out loud is powerful because when you do so it changes the nature of them. A thought spoken out loud takes internal hope and expresses it as faith.

MAKING OUR REQUESTS

"And when you pray, do not keep on babbling like pagans, for they think they will be heard because of their many words. Do not be like them, for your Father knows what you need before you ask Him." Matthew 6:7-8

A common phenomena in many prayer traditions is that of repetition[a]. This has its place but the idea that the more we repeat our request the more chance we have of God answering it is misguided. Jesus tells us

a We will explore this further in Chapter 6: Meditation

not to treat God like a lottery machine (the more tickets I buy the better chance I have of winning), but to talk to Him as if He is a benevolent parent who already knows our needs (this is echoed in the parable of the unexpected guest[a]). There is a time and place for repetition (for example, in our prayers of worship and adoration), but in the devotion of prayer we are not trying to impress God with how many times we can ask for something.

THE DESTINATION OF PRAYER

Mother Teresa[b] was once asked about her prayer life. The interviewer asked, "When you pray, what do you say to God?" Mother Teresa replied, "I don't talk, I simply listen." Believing he understood what she had just said, the interviewer next asked, "Ah, then what is it that God says to you when you pray?" Mother Teresa replied, "He also doesn't talk. He also simply listens." There was a long silence, the interviewer seemed a bit confused and didn't know what to ask next. Teresa finally broke the silence by saying, "If you can't understand the meaning of what I've just said, I'm sorry but there's no way I can explain it any better."

All those serious about plumbing the depths of prayer have eventually come to this place of contemplation.

a Luke 11:5-8, b Founder of the 'Missionaries of Charity', India

We read about it in many of the Christian classic writings on prayer. We'll learn more about this in the devotion of meditation but suffice to say here that prayer often brings us to a place of quietness; communing with God is talking, but it is also listening.

PUTTING PRAYER INTO PRACTICE

As with all the other Christian devotions, what we don't want to do is set our alarm clock for 5am, manage a couple of mornings, fall asleep during our one-hour prayer time and then give up. Think about your lifestyle as a whole and plan realistically. Think about your weekly or monthly routine and about the long term. What is a realistic goal for you to introduce a more meaningful devotional prayer rooms and times into your life?

As we've already suggested, there are a variety of ways we can get alone to do this. Perhaps factoring in a little extra time on something you already do. For example, if your commute from work to home includes passing a park area why not spend 5 minutes praying there? It doesn't have to be every day but try to make it a regular thing. It's different for everyone but I guarantee that punctuating our days with this kind of purposeful prayer activity will have a profound effect on our spiritual maturity.

Prayer is like the heartbeat of our garden because it creates space in our lives for the Lord and deepens our relationship with Him. Why not begin to make a room in your soul garden for a place of prayer?

ACTIVATION

Consider (with the Lord) how you might introduce a time of regular private prayer devotion into your lifestyle. Think 'small steps'... something achievable and sustainable. Be creative about how you could 'knit' a regular time of prayer into your daily routine. Ask yourself if there are natural opportunities in your day that might lend themselves to becoming times of prayer.

Chapter 4

fasting

the abundance of heaven

In modernity we are blessed with an abundance of food only dreamed of by our ancestors. In fact, we have a variety of food available to us that would put many a former kings' table to shame. Supermarkets provide us with year round international produce, perfectly prepared and ready to eat, picked and washed, cut and dried, butchered, baked and seasoned. A quick visit to a supermarket website brought me up 420 results for yoghurt alone! We love our take-aways to be delivered straight to our door and programmes about food: sourcing it, cooking it and eating it, are some of the most popular on TV.

It's hard to escape from the ubiquity of food and the idea of fasting for spiritual purposes seems oddly out of place in a society that practically worships it. Sure, there are fasting fads that do the rounds from time to time, you know, the one day on, one day off kind, but these are largely focussed on weight loss rather than spirituality.

WHAT IS FASTING?

Fasting is the discipline of denying ourselves the gratifying of a perfectly legitimate physical need or desire for a period of time. Traditionally in Christianity fasting has usually meant abstaining from eating food, or certain types of food, but it can include abstaining from other things too (like tv or streaming services).

So what's the benefit of fasting? Well, we all know that governing our physical needs and desires can be challenging. Watch a young child scream when it's told it can't have the chocolate bar; that's what I'm talking about. On a basic level we are all that child and fasting, perhaps more than any other devotion, teaches us to control those desires.

Fasting, when practised rightly, helps to introduce self-control and humility into other areas of our lives too. In a true fast we seek a life governed and filled by God rather than by natural desires and needs.

It's true that a legalistic approach, or too much emphasis on externals in any spiritual discipline will often make matters worse. You know what I mean; we're good for a whole week and then have a massive binge to make up for it. But what the true Christian disciplines do, including fasting, is help us to humble ourselves and better position us to receive from the Holy Spirit. We must never see disciplines like fasting as making us good in themselves, but as useful tools that assist us to be teachable and allow the Holy Spirit to do His work.

WHAT DID JESUS SAY ABOUT FASTING?

We have already seen in Matthew 6 how Jesus specifically addresses the devotions of giving and prayer, so now we come to the third devotion of fasting. Just as we have not abandoned charity or prayer as normal aspects of the Spirit-filled life we have no reason to suppose that fasting is no longer of any value. Particularly since Jesus said, *"When you fast"*, rather than *"If you fast"*.

Jesus also taught us, much like the personal devotions of charity and prayer, that fasting is to be, as much as possible, a private activity between ourselves and our Heavenly Father:

"But when you fast, put oil on your head and wash your face, so that it will not be obvious to others that you are fasting, but only to your Father, who is unseen; and your Father, who sees what is done in secret, will reward you." Matthew 6:17-18

What Jesus promises us is that what is devoted to God in private will be rewarded by God openly. Putting it another way, a personal devotion to God within your heart will manifest as the fruit of the Spirit in the outward expression of your life.

MYTH BUSTING IDEAS ABOUT FASTING

So let's address a few misconceptions about fasting:

1. It will make me into a better person

No, it won't. In the first instance it will probably make you a worse person! Who wants to be hungry! Grumpy, irritable, self-aware, and even worse: smug and self-righteous. That's the work of fasting. Just as it detoxes your liver, so many weaknesses and unpleasant traits will begin to rise to the surface. What you do with these as they emerge dictates whether fasting will be of any benefit. Only recognising and taking these 'toxins' to the cross and surrendering them to Jesus will determine whether the Holy Spirit can do His work of deepening your faith and spiritual understanding.

2. I will get ill if I miss a few meals

For anybody who is healthy, missing a few meals will not harm your body. In fact, on the contrary, there are many proven health benefits to fasting, for example, ridding the body of toxins.

However, if your doctor has advised you not to skip meals because of some health issues, there are many other forms of fasting available to you.

3. Great – fasting will help me lose weight!

Of course all calorie-controlled diets are forms of fasting, but the general medical consensus is that fasting to lose weight is not a good idea and in fact it can do harm. Besides which, we really want to focus on the spiritual with devotional fasting, so let's not get side-tracked by other agendas.

4. I won't be able to do my job

We all have different circumstances and physical demands when it comes to our occupations and we need to be sensible about what's the right kind of fast and when is best to do it. For example, If you have a heavy physical job in the construction industry you may put your safety and that of others at risk with a prolonged food fast (say, consuming nothing but fluids for over three days). However, if your job is largely sedentary, reduced food intake should not prevent you from working. The thing is to be realistic and sensible about your needs and circumstances.

However, there is a great variety of types and duration of fasting that can fit your circumstances.

5. Fasting will persuade God to do something for me

In the Christian devotion of fasting we're not in the business of 'twisting God's arm' to make Him do something for us. There is a time and a place for intercession (when we know we can pray confidently in line with God's will), but with devotional fasting we're not primarily focussing on this type of activity, but on humbling ourselves before God and allowing Him to do His work in our hearts.

A note on eating disorders

And finally, I just want to mention eating disorders such as anorexia nervosa. I would advise anyone with any kind of diagnosed eating disorder to avoid fasting. Get the ministry, counsel and help you need to get well, and be free from any debilitating eating disorder. You may be able to come back to fasting when you know you're completely free of any eating disorder problem.

FASTING PRACTICALITIES

So how do we go about the devotion of fasting? Essentially, it's not complicated. We decide what kind of fast we want to do, for how long and we get started. It's important to determine exactly what to fast from and for how long and, this is important, *stick to it*. Otherwise, it's amazing how easy it is for a fast to get compromised.

As with all the other spiritual devotions absolute secrecy may be a challenge, if not impossible. You'll probably have to tell those you live with, and maybe even those you work with. Try and keep it on a 'need to know' basis, it won't spoil your fast; God sees your heart.

When you've decided on the type of fast you're going to do (and for beginners I don't recommend anything longer than one day – in fact, perhaps just start off by skipping one meal), begin to anticipate the fast with prayer and thanksgiving. Tell God that more than anything, you are hungry for more of Him in your life.

If you're missing meals you still need plenty of liquids (food often contains water). Of course drink as much water as you like but also consider adding some fresh fruit juice or some mild herbal tea like camomile (caffeine free) to hot drinks.

Seriously consider cutting out addictive substances such as caffeine, alcohol, chocolate and high sugar drinks/snacks. In fact, just fasting from one of these (if you are a regular consumer) will likely be enough of a fast on its own. However, be aware that if you do this there can be very unpleasant withdrawal symptoms such as headaches that may take a few days to pass.

If you're in a cold climate you may need to wrap up extra warm if you are doing a prolonged food fast.

SOCIAL CONSIDERATIONS

Another practical aspect of fasting is mealtimes. For many these are social times in the kitchen and around the table; times to be with family or friends. It's perfectly possible to join in these times while fasting, perhaps with a drink.

One unfortunate side effect of fasting is bad breath. This will only be an issue in fasting that lasts 24 hours or longer because the body will begin to detox (a process whereby the body releases toxins which have built up over time). The bad breath is caused by these toxins coming out; so it's all good. Sugar free mints or gum are a good antidote.

When you break your fast have something light and nourishing like vegetable soup and fruit juice. Praise God for His goodness and for the blessing of food and provision.

FASTING: SPIRITUAL PREPARATION

If we're new to fasting it's hard not to feel just a little self-righteous if telling others about it... God is revealing our pride already and we haven't even started yet! Humble yourself and let the Holy Spirit do His work.

One thing you'll notice pretty quickly is that our days are naturally punctuated by meal times. We talk of 'lunch break', but now we're fasting it's just an 'empty break'. The obvious way to use these times is in devotional prayer or reading. Prayer and fasting combine together in a very powerful way.

Before fasting you may consider meditating on a particular scripture during the fast. How about Isaiah 58 in which the Lord rebukes Israel for the misunderstanding of fasting:

"Is not this the kind of fasting I have chosen: to loose the chains of injustice and untie the cords of the yoke,

to set the oppressed free and break every yoke?" Isaiah 58:6

It's not that fasting is wrong but that true fasting should bear this kind of fruit.

Fasting, when practised well also yields times of joy. Times of heightened revelation and union with God. It brings us into a clearer perspective; a 'God perspective'. We may experience times of deep peace and profound spiritual depth. Fasting can strip away barriers or blockages in our faith life and open up new vistas. Why not journal while you fast; the good the bad and the divine? See what God will reveal and speak into your life.

BRINGING IT ALL TOGETHER

If we imagine our life is like a garden and Jesus is our master gardener, when it comes to our soul garden perhaps fasting, more than any of the other disciplines is going to make us face up to the more unpleasant jobs around the garden.

You see, just when we thought the garden was looking lovely and fruitful our Father God is going to put His finger on those areas which we'd rather ignore. He's going to prune us back so that we can walk in more freedom and revelation of who He is in us, and bear even more fruit. Devotional fasting helps reveal some of these deep-seated areas of fear and pride so that the Lord can deal with them. If we allow God to deal with us in these times of secret honesty and vulnerability, we will find that we are able to be more honourable to Jesus in public.

Through fasting we are able to be filled with a deeper reliance on God and walk in a proven trust. It empowers us to live an overcoming life that roots us deeper into the foundation of God; a life filled with the abundance of heaven. **Isaiah 58** goes on to say:

"Then your light will break forth like the dawn, and your healing will quickly appear; then your right-eousness will go before you, and the glory of the Lord will be your rear guard. Then you will call, and the Lord will answer; you will cry for help, and He will say: Here am I."

ACTIVATION

Choose a fast and a good time to do it. Bearing in mind that there are a whole range of things you can fast from (for example, social media or tv and streaming services). However, if you can fast from food I encourage you to do so. Perhaps miss one meal to start with. Prepare for your fast by writing down *what* you intend to do and *when* so that it's clear. As usual, small steps are always best. Determine what you might do while fasting; how will you spend the time? Break the fast with gratitude and thanksgiving.

Chapter 5

worship

the treasure store

Mention 'Christian worship' to most people and they will assume you mean the gathering together of believers for an act of corporate worship. This can mean anything from singing traditional hymns, to improvised vocals on a jazz-rock fusion instrumental. Whether your preference is for the monastic chanting of Thomas Tallis or the latest hit from the Christian charts; that's often what we mean by 'worship'.

But as important as corporate expressions of worship in song and music are, worship is far more encompassing, more life embracing, than this organised expression. Worship is a lifestyle or a way of seeing life. You could say that worship is part of our identity, it defines the way we live.

THE HEART OF WORSHIP

After Jesus had taught about the importance of the private devotions of charity, prayer and fasting in Matthew 6 He went on to tell us about storing up treasure in heaven.

"Do not store up for yourselves treasures on earth, where moths and vermin destroy, and where thieves break in and steal. But store up for yourselves treasures in heaven, where moths and vermin do not destroy, and where thieves do not break in and steal. For where your treasure is, there your heart will be also."
Matthew 6:19-21

He was telling us that when we value the things of God more than the things of the world then we are truly living a life of worship. This effectively summarised His former teaching on the importance of living devotionally before God, because when we worship anything we entrust our heart to it and make it our treasure.

WHERE YOUR TREASURE IS

"Where your treasure is, there your heart will be also."[a] Treasure. That's the result of worship; to make a treasure of that which it adores.

Though, certainly in many European nations, we've

a Matthew 6:21

evicted God from society, we still see worship all around us every day. Worship is the act of bowing down to someone or something, even if that some-thing is a celebrity, personal fame and fortune or a political position or ideological belief. These are not necessarily bad in themselves, but become idols when they supercede the place of God in our lives.

The word 'worship' comes from an old English word meaning, 'an acknowledgement of worth'. We might say 'worth-ship'. To worship is to say, "You're valuable to me and you're worth it". When we do anything that honours and values the Lord, that recognises His sovereignty and authority, it's then that we are worshipping and telling Him, He's worth it. Jesus is warning us that if we invest in and sacrifice for earthly and temporary things, then what we gain will ultimately be worthless. It will only bring us distress and worry. Why? Because no matter how much wealth we accumulate it will decay or be taken from us. So, it's much better to invest in eternal treasure that benefits us both now and in the afterlife.

Essentially this teaching is an appeal to look after your heart. Don't put it in the garbage where it will get battered and bruised, put it in the Father's hands where it will be safe and protected.

How do we do that? When Jesus was asked what was the greatest commandment He replied:

"Love the Lord your God with all your heart and with all your soul and with all your mind."[a] That's worship.

REJOICE!

Over and over again the Bible tells us to rejoice in verses like Philippians 4:4:

"Rejoice in the Lord always. I will say it again: Rejoice!"

'Rejoice' is a form of the word 'joy' (re-**joi**-ce) and is mentioned over 300 times in the Bible. Joy is very different to happiness. Happiness is by nature emotional and fleeting and relies on external circumstances. There's nothing wrong with happiness, the Bible uses the word 'happy' too, but it always emphasises 'joy'. Joy is a deeper state of well-being that continues despite our circumstances; because it's anchored in faith.

"This is the day which the LORD has made; Let us rejoice and be glad in it." Psalm 118:24

Now some might say, "What's the point in that? I don't feel glad, I've got this problem and that problem! Are you asking me to be dishonest?" But the wise person responds to the deeper call of joy. Just like giving, and

a Matthew 22:37

prayer and fasting, the call to rejoice in God is a choice of the will, a discipline even, and one that can set us free from introspection and despair.

This is important in our pursuit of the spiritual devotions because otherwise we're always in danger of becoming far too sombre and serious, but the goal of the devotional life is freedom and joy. That's why Psalm 103 says, **"Bless the Lord oh my soul"**[a], because we have to tell ourselves (our soul), to be glad; "Come on soul - get praising!" and remind ourselves of God's goodness and faithfulness.

WORSHIP IN THE BIBLE

Throughout the Bible there are many different Hebrew words used for different kinds of worship - but the meaning is often lost in the English translations. Here's just a few:

YADAH - meaning 'open hands to God' - the first time it's used in scripture is when Jacob's wife Leah has her fourth child and calls him Judah. She says, 'now I will **praise** (yadah) the Lord (open my hands to Him)'[b].

HALAL - to noisily boast about God, be joyful, to shine. It's where we get the word Hallelujah. Literally **halal** (boast joyfully about) Yahweh.

a Psalm 103:1, b Genesis 29:35

SHABACH - is a joyful and loud testimony of what God has done. In Psalms 145:4 "one generation shall **praise** (shabach) Your works to another, and shall declare Your mighty acts."

BARAUCH - is submission through the act of kneeling. A complete surrender of ourselves to God. In 1 Chronicles 29:20 we read that King David **blessed** the Lord and all the people **blessed** the Lord and fell prostrate on the floor. The word blessed there is '**barauch**'.

ZAMAR - Praise that is sung with instruments. So far none of these worship words are specifically musical but this one is. So, in Psalm 144:1,9 "Praise be (barauch) to the Lord my Rock, who trains my hands for war, and my fingers for battle... I will sing a new song to You, O God; On a harp of ten strings I will **make music** (zamar) to You."

RINNAH - joyfully proclaim. Let them sacrifice thank offerings and **tell** (rinnah) of His works with songs of joy.[a]

TEHILLAH - HALAL that is sung. Believe it or not the first Halal we looked at is only spoken, but spoken in a loud, "I'm crazy for God" way. But Tehillah is when this kind of passion gets combined with music and sung. So - "Enter into His gates with thanksgiving and into His courts with **praise** (tehillah)" Psalm 100:4.

a Psalm 107:22

EXPRESS YOURSELF

There's a place for being quiet and still in our worship of God, but there's also a place for shouting and jumping for joy! Imagine King David as a boy in the wilderness caring for the sheep. Do you think he was still before God when he worshipped Him there? I don't think so; not judging by the kind of worshipper David grew up to be[a]. David was an ecstatic worshipper; he danced with all his might. Just as he killed the lion and bear in private before he killed Goliath in public[b], I believe he also learned how to sing, play and worship God in the desert before he danced and praised God in public.

The tabernacle that David established was a place of 24/7 worship: a place of music, joy and creativity[c]. Amos prophesied that David's tabernacle would be restored[d], and the Apostles later said this was being fulfilled by the outpouring of the Holy Spirit on both Jew and Gentile[e]. We are the temple of the Holy Spirit[f]; we have become that extravagant place of worship.

IT'S JUST NOT ME

Now, some readers may be bristling at the suggestion that worship can be extravagant and expressive. And I get it, I really do! I have been in those meetings where we are encouraged to clap, or jump, or even dance in a

a 2 Samuel 6:14, b 1 Samuel 17:34-36, c 1 Chronicles 16, d Amos 9:11
e Acts 15:12-18, f 1 Cor 6:19

church service. But this is different. For a start, we're talking about private personal devotions here so there is no (human) audience; just you and God (and maybe a few angels). If you feel awkward or gawky or inelegant, who cares? No one knows! Secondly, our journey into five classic Christian disciplines is all about pushing some boundaries and exploring new ways to deepen our faith in God. Trying something new is what it's all about. And finally, did you know that one of the few times that sacrifice is mentioned in the New Testament is regarding 'praise':

"Through Jesus, therefore, let us continually offer to God a sacrifice of praise—the fruit of lips that openly profess His name." Hebrews 13:15

Sacrifices are not sacrifices unless they cost you something, and in this case it could be that you need to set aside your preconceived 'preferences' and begin to move your body in new expressions of praise.

SOMETHING TO TRY

During a study into the threefold blessing of God[a] I formulated a simple prayer/act of worship that I use as part of my devotional times.

Firstly stand with hands raised to heaven and say:

a 'The Threefold Miracle Mandate' 55:11 Publishing

"Father God, you are the creator of the heavens and the earth."

Then open your arms to the sides, palms up and say:

"Jesus you are the saviour of the world."

And finally kneel and say,

"Holy Spirit you are all-powerful and all-present."

Then repeat the three stances saying:

"Father God, because you are my shepherd I lack no good thing."

"Jesus because you are my saviour I am forgiven and fully accepted."

"Holy Spirit because I serve you I am significant in my servanthood whatever you call me to do."

THE EYE IS THE LAMP

"The eye is the lamp of the body. If your eyes are healthy, your whole body will be full of light. But if your eyes are unhealthy, your whole body will be full of darkness. If then the light within you is darkness, how great is that darkness!" Matthew 6:22-23

After talking about storing up treasure in heaven, Jesus says a curious thing. He says the eye is the lamp of the body. What does He mean? He says that if your eyes are good then your whole body will be full of light but if your eyes are bad then the light within you will be darkness.

Jesus is speaking symbolically. He's not talking about physical eyes and or even physical light. When He says '**eyes**' He means our perception or the way we see the world, and when He says '**light**' he means our revelation or understanding.

This follows on from His teaching on personal devotions because when we engage in these activities (as worship to God), Jesus is saying that we will actually change the way we think and see. It's how we engage in the renewing of the mind (eyes or perception) and let the light (revelation) in:

"Do not conform to the pattern of this world, but be transformed by the renewing of your mind. Then you will be able to test and approve what God's will is - His good, pleasing and perfect will." Romans 12:2

Worship is how we break free from our old ways of thinking, from the prison thinking of legalism and licence that we considered in the introduction. Jesus warns us that unless our perception changes then we will live under a delusion; our light will be darkness. In other words, the way we see the world will be flawed and corrupt.

KNOWING GOD'S PRESENCE

When we worship the Lord, He may manifest His presence in a very special way; often in a way that we can feel or sense. Many times, people will describe this feeling as a thick blanket of peace or deep joy. What happens when we apply ourselves to worshipping God in all these diverse ways, (not only in times of corporate song, but also in private proclamation, in shouting, in hands opened and jumping or kneeling), is that we enter, by faith, through His gates and into His heavenly courts.

"Enter his gates with thanksgiving and His courts with praise; give thanks to Him and praise His name." Psalm 100:4

It's not so much that 'God is turning up', but far more that we are presenting ourselves to Him. Cultivating the devotion or discipline of worship **'sets our minds on things above'**[a] like no other activity will. Worship changes everything because it establishes the power of God over and in our lives like nothing else can.

a Colossians 3:2

AUTHENTIC WORSHIP

God created and enjoys the richness and variety of life[a] and He loves all acts of worship[b]. Get in the secret place, close the door to your 'room' (whether that's inside your home or out in the country) and express worship to God in positions and movements of reverence, submission, joy and celebration. Have you ever done that? It's very liberating! When we are free to jump and shout and kneel and lie on the ground in our own personal worship of God, then we are free indeed. The joy of the Lord will be our strength and it will permeate our days. Submission and deference to God will flow naturally into our lifestyle. We will feel more secure and confident because our hearts will be safe, right there where our treasure is, in the hands of our loving heavenly Father.

a Genesis 1 & 2, b John 4:23

ACTIVATION

Remember all those Hebrew words for expressions of worship we looked at in this chapter (pages 65-66)? Get on your own and, as an expression of worship, begin to make some noise! In your personal devotional time, whether inside or out, engage in a variety of joyful expressions of worship. Try shouting praise, noisily boast about God's goodness, raise your hands and move around. For some this may be very stretching but also surprisingly liberating... don't disregard this discipline until you have tried it!

Chapter 6

meditation

living in the present

In 1934 T S Eliot wrote a poem called 'Choruses from the Rock'. Here's an extract:

The endless cycle of idea and action,
Endless invention, endless experiment,
Brings knowledge of motion, but not of stillness;
Knowledge of speech, but not of silence;
Knowledge of words, and ignorance of the Word.

It was a prophetic poem in a century that saw the application of innovation explode upon the world. Flight, cars, telephony, cinema, television, computers and internet. We even put a man on the moon. But in all this activity and progress Eliot asks:

Where is the Life we have lost in living?

Where is the wisdom we have lost in knowledge?
Where is the knowledge we have lost in information?

CHRISTIANITY IS A RELATIONSHIP

In its essence Christianity is a relationship. Jesus said,

"Now this is eternal life: that they know you, the only true God, and Jesus Christ, whom you have sent." John 17.3

This is the wisdom and knowledge that T S Eliot feared we were losing in our endless cycle of idea and innovation: experiencing the real relational knowledge of God in our hearts. This special relationship with God isn't based on any physical ability of our bodies or the intellectual skill of our brain; which is good to know isn't it? Because God is spirit, rather, it's a matter for the spirit: our spirit communing and knowing God's Spirit. Deep calling to deep[a].

From around the 5th Century AD in the medieval west, Christianity was nurtured in an atmosphere of commitment and devotion in monasteries and nunneries. The goal was not the pursuit of knowledge for its own sake, but edification and worship, contemplation, and adoration of God through a lifestyle of devotion. The theologian was not a detached observer but a

a Psalm 42:7

committed involved participant. The highest goal was relational knowledge of God.

However, by the 11th century it had become more important to be a philosopher than to be a godly man as Universities birthed scholastic theology, the goal of which was objective intellectual knowledge. Within academic theology, though God's existence was not questioned until much later on, the idea that one could truly know or experience God began to be challenged. By the nineteenth century the German philosopher Friedrich Nietzsche famously lamented that the enlightenment or 'age of science and reason' had 'killed God': "What was holiest and mightiest of all that the world has yet owned has bled to death under our knives: who will wipe this blood off us?[a]"

As Paul says in Romans: **'their thinking became futile and their foolish hearts were darkened. Although they claimed to be wise, they became fools.'** [b]

The discipline of meditation helps us to come away from what T S Eliot called 'Knowledge of words, and ignorance of the Word' and come back to a place of deep understanding. To lay down our vain attempts at theological logic and reasoning and know in our heart and soul that He is God[c].

a The Joyful Pursuit of Knowledge and Understanding 1882, b Romans 1:22 c Psalm 46:10

MEDITATION IN THE BIBLE

Meditation is mentioned many times in the Bible and Strong's Concordance translates several Hebrew words as 'meditate'. They are Hebrew words that are associated with muttering, chewing and murmuring and they suggest an act of repetitious speaking. Here's a couple of scriptures that contain the words 'meditate':

Joshua 1:8: 'This Book of the Law shall not depart from your mouth, but you shall meditate on it day and night'

And **Psalm 104: 'May my meditation be pleasing to him, for I rejoice in the Lord.'**

And in the New Testament we are told to 'dwell' or 'settle our thoughts' on good things:

'If there is any excellence and if anything worthy of praise, dwell on these things.' Philippians 4:8

The Bible doesn't tell us how to meditate because in ancient Arabic culture the practice would have been commonplace. So, when Genesis 24 tells us that **'Isaac went out to meditate in the field toward evening'** what was he doing? What exactly is meditating and how does it help us?

EASTERN MEDITATION

We need to beware and guard against becoming involved in popular forms of eastern meditation. Yoga, though principally a physical activity, is also a form of meditation. The word yoga means 'to yoke'. It's an expression of the linking of the human soul with 'the universal soul'. Many of the positions in yoga are 'moving mantras' and rooted in worship of deities. Likewise in modern transcendental meditation the goal is often self discovery or self fulfilment but it's methods and roots are based around many ancient Hindu beliefs and writings.

Biblical and Christian meditation are quite different from these Eastern practices. One of the essential differences is that in many Eastern forms of meditation those who meditate seek to 'empty' themselves whereas the goal of Christian meditation is to be filled with the Word and with the Spirit. Some may argue that meditation has no place in Christian practice but, just as we do not reject the practices of giving, prayer or fasting because they appear in other religions, neither should we reject Biblical meditation for this reason alone.

THE BENEFITS OF MEDITATION

You may already meditate without realising it; even

though you may not be aware of it. Did you know that worrying is a form of meditation? The same thought repeating over and over again without any deviation or resolve; always returning to the same stream of thought. That's a kind of negative meditation. Worrying is just meditating on the wrong thing.

What the Christian discipline of meditation does is take control of those toxic or runaway thoughts. Our heads can be jumbled full of them; you know, that 'stream of consciousness conversation' that chatters away all the time; much of it fruitless worry. Meditation helps to bring our chattering mind to a quiet rest so that the Holy Spirit can fill our hearts and open our spiritual ears.

Meditation is also scientifically proven to have some moderate health benefits[a]. One of the greatest health challenges of our time is stress and anxiety and their devastating affects on our lives. Meditation helps to reduce stress and can improve cognitive abilities such as attention span and memory[b].

MEDITATION COMPLEMENTS BIBLE STUDY

We have already seen that there are many verses in the Bible about meditating on God's law or on the Word of God. Bible meditation is different from Bible study

a Meditation programs for psychological stress and well-being:
  a systematic review and meta-analysis. JAMA Intern Med.
b On mind wandering, attention, brain networks, and meditation -
  Amit Sood / David T Jones

because it doesn't primarily seek an intellectual understanding; it seeks a deeper knowledge, a heart knowledge. Meditating on the Bible will complement your Bible study in an enriching way because the Holy Spirit will bring fresh revelation to you through a richer, more spiritual understanding.

The discipline of Bible meditation is repetition and memorisation of words from the scriptures repeated over and over again without moving on. This is what is meant by meditating. It's like chewing on food, which in many ways the Word of God is to our souls.

THE OBJECT OF OUR MEDITATIONS

Take a passage (the simpler the better) such as this one from Matthew 5:

"Blessed are the meek, for they will inherit the earth."

We know this verse is packed with truth and meaning but in meditation we're not extracting that meaning, we're simply focussing on the words. We repeat them over and over until we've memorised them. And then... and then we keep repeating them. And then we keep repeating them some more...

"But Rob, that will get boring." Yes, it will; *for your intellect*. But you must believe that something else is happening. You are bringing your thoughts into the rhythm and cadence of God's living word. It's like breathing in and out.

We don't meditate in a vacuum; in meditation we seek God's presence. In his book 'The celebration of Discipline' Richard Foster wrote: "Meditation is threatening to us because it boldly calls us to enter into the living presence of God for ourselves. It tells us that God is speaking in the continuous present and wants to address us. It's not just for the elite but for everyone."

MEDITATING ON CREATION

The Psalms are full of exhortations to meditate on God's word, but they also encourage us to meditate on His works, His creation.

"I will meditate on all Your work and muse on Your deeds." Psalm 77:12

The celebrated artist Vincent Van Gogh said, "It is looking at things for a long time that ripens you and gives you a deeper understanding." When was the last time you stopped to sit and really look at the world around you? You may say, "Well Rob, I'd love to just stop and do nothing, but I haven't got time." And if that's really true then see meditation as a challenge;

these devotional activities are called disciplines for a reason, they don't come easy and they're not quick fixes. For most of us, if we just traded 15 minutes of watching TV for 15 minutes of devotional time it would be a good start.

And so, we can see God's handiwork in the golden sunrise and the deep orange sunset, the sparkling rain drops and the aromatic flowers of the garden. Perhaps that's what Isaac was doing when he went out to the field to meditate. Remember there was no written word of God for him then, no Torah, no Psalms or book of Proverbs; but there was the glory of creation that speaks of God's glory.

HOW TO MEDITATE

Meditation is very easy to understand but difficult to master. Here's a basic guide:

1. Find a comfortable, quiet place (not too comfortable), inside or outside. Sitting with legs uncrossed and hands resting on your thighs.

2. Let your breathing begin to slow and deepen. Feel your diaphragm and belly rise and fall and become more aware of your breathing. Breathe in through your nose and out through your mouth.

3. Begin to focus on a simple scripture or Biblical truth by repetition. For example, breathe in 'Christ in me'[a] and breathe out 'Me in Christ'[b].

4. The heart of the discipline is to bring your wandering mind back within this simple channel every time it wanders.

5. Try and do this for 5 minutes (or more depending on experience). If you are new to meditation you will feel like 5 minutes is an age because you are not used to the lack of thought stimulation, but persevere and master your impulse to give up.

6. Then sit quietly and wait upon the Lord.

7. Give thanks.

The key to succeeding in any discipline is to set your heart on the long term but, at the same time, enjoy the activity. Press through the initial feelings of boredom and lack of results. This is not a quick test but a long term investment.

A few more tips:

1. In devotional meditation solitude is important. You may establish (over repeated use) a special place to meditate (inside or out).

a Colossians 1:27, b Colossians 3:3

2. The subject of our meditation is crucial, the simpler the better. It could be a scripture, a single word, a landscape, or a single leaf.

3. Your mind will wander. You will think of a million jobs to do. Many of us really don't know how to be still, we can only switch off by occupying our minds with entertainment; video streaming, music, puzzles, novels. Take charge of your thoughts. Bring them back to the subject as many times as it takes.

4. Biblical or Christian Meditation yields precious long term fruit. At times you may experience a deep joy of God's presence and at others you may not. What matters is that we **'make every effort to enter Gods rest'**[a] and be present in the moment. This will enrich your life on every level; body, spirit and soul.

SUMMARY

At the end of Matthew chapter 6 Jesus says that the world runs about in frantic activity after provision and security, but we are to be those who pursue God's Kingdom and His righteousness. It's not that provision and security are not important to God; they are, and He promises to fulfil all those needs; but only through our complete trust in Him.

a Hebrews 4:11

The discipline of meditation is one of the most precious of all the Christian disciplines because it helps us to stop. Not just on the outside, like we do when we're relaxing; but stop on the inside as well. It's a mistake to think that 'doing nothing' is resting. Doing nothing when our hearts and minds are racing away is not resting, in fact it's exhausting. That's why many would rather keep occupied. But Meditation helps us to rest on the inside too, to enter into the peace of God; to know His rest in the garden of our soul.

"So there remains a Sabbath rest for the people of God. For whoever enters God's rest also rests from his own work, just as God did from His." Hebrews 4:9

It's tragic to be so caught up in the business of life that we forget to live it. So preoccupied with the future that we are never in the present. Children don't have that problem, have you ever noticed that? If a child wants to do something it wants to do it right now! 'In 5 minutes' has no meaning for a child. They live in the present. Perhaps that's one of the reasons Jesus said **'unless you change and become like little children, you will never enter the kingdom of heaven.' Matthew 18:3**

Because it's when we are really present in the moment, the here and now, that we really meet with God and truly 'know the Word'.

ACTIVATION

Find a quiet, comfortable place to meditate. As the subject of your meditation take the twofold statement of our unity with Christ: 'Christ in me - me in Christ' (see page 84). As you breathe in say (or think) 'Christ in me', and as you breathe out, say (or think) 'me in Christ'.

Allow your breathing to go slower and deeper and allow the truth of this spiritual reality to become your one focus. If your thoughts begin to wander bring them back to this single phrase. If you are new to meditation challenge yourself to practice this for five minutes.

When you have finished, remain in a place of quiet for a couple more minutes, and then give thanks.

Chapter 7

devotions

a tree of life

We've walked the ancient pathways taken by so many others who've gone before us: charity, prayer, fasting, worship and meditation. They are pathways that help bring us into the freedom of the gospel. These activities all interact and complement one another.

When we **fast** it draws us naturally into times of **prayer** and **worship**. **Prayers** of intercession and forgiveness cultivate a lifestyle of **charity** and generosity to others. Our expressions of **worship** and joy lead us into times of peace and **meditation** where we are fully present with God. Though we can define the devotions in emphasis, we can't separate them in their purpose. They are tools that we can learn to use skilfully to help us grow up into the things of God.

THE TWOFOLD WORK OF GOD

The work of God in our lives is twofold. It is complete and it's also developing or maturing. It's complete and perfect because God has planted in us a new nature; a perfect divine nature:

"For you have been born again, not of perishable seed, but of imperishable, through the living and enduring word of God." 1 Peter 1:23

This is because when we are born again by the Spirit we become children of God and enter into eternal life.

"Yet to all who did receive Him, to those who believed in His name, he gave the right to become children of God" John 1:12

The Greek word *'teknon'* is used here in John 1:12 and means 'child' or we could say, 'new believer'. Your divine nature is perfect and needs nothing adding to it, but it also needs to grow and mature; and that's the second part of the salvation work of God.

That's why the the Greek word *'huios'* is also used in passages like Galatians 4:7: **"Therefore you are no longer a slave but a son"**. The word translated 'son' here is *huios*, which refers to fully mature children who inherit the Kingdom of God.

The Lord God wants to work with us to see that new nature, that imperishable seed, grow from a child (teknon) into a great tree, coming into full maturity (huios). The five personal devotions we have explored in this series are like tools that can help us play our part in this work. Why? Because it is through practising devotions like giving, prayer and fasting that we can help tend that divine life.

This is what it means to **"work out our salvation"**[a], to reverently devote ourselves to help cultivate what God has planted in us, so that we will become mature and reach the whole measure of the fullness of Jesus[b]. Our discipleship must contain a measure of discipline, and so we express our love of God through the self-control of a devoted life. Just as we would apply ourselves to excel at a musical instrument we do so to excel in godliness:

"All athletes are disciplined in their training. They do it to win a prize that will fade away, but we do it for an eternal prize." 1 Corinthians 9:25

Our training may begin as a challenge but the practise and reward soon becomes a joy.

Let's have a brief recap of the five devotions we have looked at in this book:

a Philippians 2:12, b Ephesians 4:13

CHARITY: The overflowing life

We began with charity, or 'the overflowing life'. In the Bible this is often translated as the English word love, but charity is not emotional or romantic love, it's 'agape love' or 'divine love' that gives selflessly. Love for God which then overflows in love for others[a] is central to the devotions because, as Paul reminds us:

**"And now these three remain: faith, hope and (agape) love. But the greatest of these is (agape) love."
1 Corinthians 13:13**

Practising a devotional lifestyle of agape love is more than just being generous with money; it's a lifestyle of servanthood. Honouring others, just as Jesus honoured us, no matter who they may be, as valuable people. This is a great leveller as we see grace may flow through us to others regardless of status or merit.

We can learn to be intentional with our time and money by offering these up to God in our personal devotions and asking for His guidance on how best to use our resources. We are to be good stewards of our finances and move beyond 'responsive giving' to 'guided giving' when it comes to using them to bless others. As John Bunyan said "You have not lived today until you have done something for someone who can

a Matthew 22:36-40

never repay you." Through this devotion we open up our hearts to receive and release the flow of the Father's love. Charity or agape love is the heartbeat of our soul garden.

PRAYER: The secret groves

Our recognition of God's great grace in our lives leads us away from the crowds and into the secret groves of devotional prayer; the place of intimacy with God. God's faithfulness to us finds a reverberation in our spoken prayers of adoration, supplication and repentance. Prayer is the first step of faith-action that releases God's Kingdom on the earth. **"Your kingdom come, your will be done, on earth as it is in heaven"**[a].

In prayer we honour the Father; we trust Him for provision; we pray for strength and protection. We also release ourselves into the Father's forgiveness, as at the same time, we release others from their offences against us.

Learning how to knit personal 'prayer rooms' into our daily lives is essential for developing spiritual maturity. Devotional prayer is entering into the throne room of God, it's a priestly appointment of privilege under our high priest Jesus. **"The prayers of a righteous person are powerful and effective"**[b].

a Matthew 6:10, b James 5:16

FASTING: The abundance of heaven

FASTING gives us deep roots of hope. When there is a dry season a tree's roots go deeper as they hope for living waters. Fasting teaches us how to push into the things of God and become more anchored in Him. Fasting effectively unearths and reveals our weaknesses, weaknesses that God can deal with if we let Him. It enables us to leave the wilderness in the power of the Holy Spirit[a].

In fasting we deny the flesh and look to the return of the Bridegroom saying, **"Maranatha, come Lord Jesus"**[b], because He is the author and finisher of our salvation. It's through the devotion of fasting we honour God as our sole provider and unlock the abundance of heaven. This devotion will develop deep spiritual roots in us like no other.

WORSHIP: The treasure store

As well as faith, hope and love[c] the Bible also speaks of love, joy and peace[d]. Together these Christian virtues form a fivefold circle of devotions with love at the centre. In the personal devotion of worship we experience the mountain tops of celebration in God. This yields a deep and lasting joy that remains through all circumstances.

a Luke 4:14, b Revelation 22:20, c 1 Corinthians 13:13, d Galatians 5:22

Throughout the Bible we see personal expressions of worship that include shouting and bragging about God, the 'yadah' of opening hands to Him, and the loud testimony of what God has done. Most of these acts of worship are not set to music or in public gatherings but expressed in the highs, lows and variety of everyday life.

From the 'barach' of reverent kneeling to the exhilaration of 'tehillah', devotional worship sets us free from taking ourselves too seriously. It brings us into the freedom of joy.

MEDITATION: Living in the present

And finally, after our pilgrimage, we sat down and contemplated meditation. A devotion that brings a halt to the frantic chatter of our thought life and brings us into the present moment with God. A powerful discipline that sets us free from toxic worry and brings us into His peace and rest.

Meditation helps orientate our lives to the Holy Spirit as well as benefiting our physical and mental health. It brings us into the present where we can enter the rest of God; His eternal presence. Those who practice meditating on the word and life of God are cultivating a **'mind set on things above'**[a] and who are able to know the will of God[b].

a Colossians 3:1, b Romans 12:2

THE TREE OF LIFE

All these devotions have been practiced by believers ever since time began. Even in the garden of Eden we see all these aspects of life in God for Adam and Eve. The river of divine love, the speaking with God in the cool of the evening, the abundant provision of God in the trees of the garden, the joy of fruitfulness and purpose and the peace of God in Sabbath rest.

Perhaps all these virtues are summed up in the tree of life; a mysterious symbol of the life of Christ in the heart of the garden. To eat of this tree was to eat of eternal life. When we are born again it is this tree that God wants to grow and mature in the garden of our souls.

GROWING UP INTO MATURITY

When we were children there was a responsibility on those around us to help us and look after us. In the same way, those who are ahead of us in the things of God can help guide us and instruct us. However, we shouldn't stay in the nursery forever.

**"When I was a child, I talked like a child, I thought like a child, I reasoned like a child. When I became a man, I put the ways of childhood behind me."
1 Corinthians 13:11**

When we are 'new Christians' we are like a young sapling that needs tending by others. If it's dry weather our spiritual parents can go to the stream and get water to quench our thirst. But as we read in Psalm 1, our destiny is to be like **'a tree planted by streams of water, which yields its fruit in season and whose leaf does not wither'**. This is a picture of a child becoming a mature son by drinking from the river of life for themselves. The promise for that God-centred life is for health, fruitfulness and true prosperity[a].

Growing up takes time and effort. It's not necessarily a question of sin, but desiring to walk in the light as much as possible[b]. The scriptures say that even Jesus had to learn obedience[c], which is a great reassurance to us. To learn wisdom and responsibility means being willing to persevere, with the Holy Spirit at every step as our counsellor and guide[d].

PRIVATE DEVOTION AND PUBLIC POWER

It's worth repeating as we conclude this journey through these five classic Christian devotions that practising them won't make God love us any more than He already does. Even if we did nothing else in our lives to pursue God, He wouldn't love us any less. What these devotional activities will do is increase our

a Psalm 1:3, b 1 John 1:7, c Hebrew 5:8, d John 14:16

capacity to receive and express that love. They will nurture the seeds of life that God has sown into our hearts. And in turn they will help us be a conduit for that love to flow out to others.

There is a profound relationship between our private life and our public life. Between love and power. Jesus Himself entered the 'private' wilderness of prayer and fasting before he entered the public domain of ministry 'in the power of the Spirit'. And so I am persuaded that as we become those who know God deeper, the power of the Spirit will begin to manifest more in our lives; it's simply the (super)natural result of true spiritual maturity. And this is not for our own sake, but all in the Lord's service and for His glory as we become:

Those who through giving know how to love and be loved.

Those who through faithful prayer know God's faithfulness.

Those who through fasting know the sure hope of resurrection.

Those who through devotional worship know the joy of the Lord as their strength.

And those who through meditation know the present reality of God's peace and rest.

"Because the wisdom that comes from heaven is first of all pure; then peace-loving, considerate, submissive, full of mercy and good fruit, impartial and sincere. Peacemakers who sow in peace reap the fruit of righteousness." James 3:17-18

ACTIVATION

Our goal is to weave these devotions into our daily routines so that they become part of the fabric of our lifestyle. There is a place for taking time out, perhaps at a dedicated retreat centre for days at a time, but here we want to focus on 'little-and-often'. Because our 'big ideas' are often the ones we never get round to or never manage to see through.

Consider the five devotions: charity, prayer, fasting, worship and meditation. Which of these areas do you think is weakest for you? Which of these areas would you like to progress in? Focus on that one over the coming weeks. If we can progress in just one area, it will often strengthen all the others too.

afterword

When I was 17 years old a family friend lent me a small green paperback book called 'The Celebration of Discipline' by Richard Foster. It was 1983, I was at High School in the 'Lower Sixth Form' and it was the holidays. I had never heard of the book, I hadn't even asked to borrow it; they just thought I might enjoy it.

I thought the style was a little challenging. There were lots of esoteric quotes from ancient saints I'd never heard of before. But it was also very practical and that caught my attention. Before long I was heading out to the countryside (our village was surrounded by farm-land) to practice some of the disciplines described in the book, like meditation, solitude, and fasting.

It was like a rite of passage, taking me from a fairly immature 'follow along' kind of faith to a more intentional pursuit of God. The big difference it made to my life was that instead of relying on others for my spiritual sustenance I was learning how to truly draw on the deep wells of the Spirit for myself. It was like an exciting adventure and the best part was, nobody else knew; it was just me and God.

Of course, over time, others did begin to notice because I began to change (in a good way). It impacted my family life, my church life and my friendships at school. Friends started to ask me about my faith and I began to be more confident about sharing it. But the best thing was, this wasn't a 'one week wonder', it was a slow, authentic change brought on by personal devotion and the Spirit's work in my heart.

Living out my faith wasn't all plain sailing from then on. Like all young adults I still had all the challenges of navigating my way to independence in the world. But even in the spiritually dark and rebellious time of my University years, that experience remained a light to guide me home.

I hope that this little book may have helped you similarly discover a deeper, more authentic faith that will bear great light and fruit. If you enjoyed this book you might also like 'A Celebration of Discipline' (which has 12 disciplines) as it has truly become a modern day Christian classic.

about the author

Rob Cresswell along with his wife Aliss pioneer ministries which seek to engage people where they are and demonstrate the love and power of God.

Rob received Jesus as his personal saviour in 1976 at the age of ten during a 'Come Together' gospel concert in Derbyshire UK.

After graduating from ministry school in 2006 they established a local church in their home town of Chester and several exciting outreach initiatives (known for salvations, healings and miracles) including a café, shop and B&B.

In 2014 they founded **Spirit Lifestyle**, a training and equipping organisation focussing on the gifts of the Spirit utilising online multimedia resources for peer to peer evangelism and discipleship training.

Rob & Aliss continue to write, present, train and travel, spreading the gospel and pioneering Kingdom initiatives internationally.

Six Essentials for Survival:

Watch Rob present

The **Believer's Guide** to
THRIVING
—— *Video Series* ——

on
SpiritLifestyle.com

More Books from
Rob & Aliss Cresswell

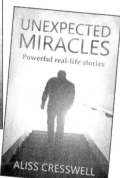

Training in
Supernatural Living

with Rob & Aliss Cresswell

- ▶ **Video Library:** instant access to quality training
- 👥 **Members Community:** for friendship and support
- 🔊 **Monthly Livestream Q&A:** with Rob & Aliss
- 🎞 **Weekly Classes:** coaching for spirit, soul and body
- ☺ **Name Your Amount:** subscription & free trial
- 🍽 **PLUS!** Local classes and cafés

We'd love to see you! *Rob + Aliss.*

SpiritLifestyle.com

miracle.cafe
a taste of heaven

For all the latest news and
stories from our Miracle Cafés

www.miracle.cafe

@miraclecafes